PRECISION TRADING WITH STEVENSON PRICE AND TIME TARGETS

J.R. STEVENSON

Traders Press, Inc.®
PO Box 6206
Greenville, SC 29606

Serving Traders Since 1975
http://www.traderspress.com

ISBN: 0-934380-94-5

Editor: Maria Dobson

Layout and Cover Design by: Teresa Darty Alligood
Traders Press, Inc.®

Traders Press, Inc.®
PO Box 6206
Greenville, SC 29606

Serving Traders Since 1975
http://www.traderspress.com

TABLE OF CONTENTS

Terms and Abbreviations Used in This Manual
Important Information
What This Manual Will or Will Not Do For You
Publisher's Foreword
Introduction

The Farmer and the Mule	1
Overview of Concepts	3
Chart 1	4
Chart 2	5
Chart 3	6
Chart 4	7
Regular and Inverted Cycles	9
Chart 5: Regular Cycles in an Uptrend	10
Chart 6: Inverted Cycles in an Uptrend	11
Chart 7: Regular and Inverted Cycles in a Downtrend	12
Concept #1: PTT [Price and Time Target]	13
Units	15
Procedure for Making a PTT in Real Time	17
How to Trade PTT's in Real Time	19
Concept #2: CTL [Cyclic Trend Line]	21
Chart 8: Concept 2	23
Chart 9: Concept 2	24
How to Select the Best Cycle to Trade	25
How to Tell When a Cycle Has Ended	27
What if the PTT Misses?	29
Basic Questions	31
Chart 10: Failure and Success	33
Chart 11	34
Chart 12	35
Chart 13: Real Time Analysis for a PTT	36
Chart 14: Results from Previous Chart	37
Chart 15: Cycles in the Pre-Market Chart	38
Chart 16: Concept 2	39
Chart 17: Real Time Trading	40
Chart 18	41
Chart 19: As the Day Progressed	43
Chart 20: Multiple Bars at the Same Chart Point	44
About Cycles	45
Chart 21: Counting Bars	47
Chart 22: Guidance Through the Day	48
Chart 23: Current Update	49
Cycles	50
Cycle Units	51
Trading Tips	53
Points of Emphasis in this Manual	55
Summary	57
Testimonials	59

Terms and Abbreviations Used In This Manual

PTT—**Price and Time Target**

TR—**Trend**-the general direction that the price is moving

TL—**Trend Line** drawn between two or more points

DT—**Double Top** - Two or more price bars that have approximately the same price highs.

DB—**Double Bottom** - Two or more price bars with approximately the same price low.

SR—**Spike Reverse** - A higher high and a lower close near the low of the bar; or a lower low and a higher close with the close near the high of the bar.

MP—**Midpoint** of a bar

RB—**Reversal Bar** - A higher high with a lower close or a lower low with a higher close. Often is seen at a PTT.

PT—**Point** - if a high point, there will be a lower price bar on each side of the high bar. If a low point, there will be a higher price bar on each side of the low bar. Note: the low or high bar can have two or more bars with equal price high or low bars.

IP—**Implied Point** - A point that develops between two or more high points or between two or more low points that may not have a point as described above. Will show an example of this as we get into the manual. See chart 14.

CYC—**Cycle** - As used in this manual, a cycle is defined as the price action that develops between two low points or between two high points.

CL—**Cycle Length** - The number of price bars between any two low points or between any two high points.

CT—**Cycle Top** - The high point between any two low points.

CB—**Cycle Bottom** - The low point between any two high points.

RC—**Regular Cycle** - Has two low points with a high point in between.

IC—**Inverted Cycle** - Has two high points with a low point in between.

UNIT—Regular cycle followed by an inverted cycle: or an inverted cycle followed by a regular cycle. [Many examples will be illustrated]

RU—**Regular Unit** - If analysis starts at a low point on a regular cycle, it is a RU. A RU is always labeled A-B-C-D.

IU—**Inverted Unit** - If analysis starts at a high point on an inverted cycle, it is an IU. An IU is always labeled B-C-D-A.

CTL—A parallel trend line (Cyclic Trend Line) to the basic trend line BTL that normally touches only one price bar, as used in Concept #2.

BTL—**Basic Trend Line,** as used in Concept #2, drawn from point B to point C on a regular cycle or a trend line drawn from point C to point D on an inverted cycle. This BTL is then cloned to get the Cyclic Trend Line (CTL.)

IMPORTANT INFORMATION

Trading the e-mini futures has large potential profit possibility but also large potential losses. You must be aware of the risks and be willing to limit your losses with the use of stops. The concepts presented in this manual are to be considered additional tools to aid you in your trading experience. The PTT's have absolutely no influence on the price action and are to be considered as markers or sign posts as to where the market may trade as a result of a certain cycle market. Properly used, they should help in your analysis of the market that you are trading.

Past results are not necessarily an indication of future results. However, all examples in this manual, except the GE stock example, were selected after this manual was started, to show that the concepts were valid in the markets that are ahead. Current examples will be shown on any future printings of this manual.

There is no guarantee or assurance that your e-mini trading will be profitable. You are responsible for your own trading decisions.

WHAT THIS MANUAL WILL OR WILL NOT DO FOR YOU

1. On a 5 minute chart of Mini S&P's, you will be able to look ahead 20, 30, 60 or even several hours and predict where the price should be at a certain time. [PTT]

2. You will be able to tell which cycles are moving the market trend.

3. You will be able to give a PTT for any cycle from 3 bars on up in length.

4. You will be able to reduce your trading to just a few trades per session to prevent over-trading, if you desire.

5. You will be able to tell when a reaction, or a rally against the trend is about to stop.

6. You will see why chart patterns form and how PTT's can confirm their targets.

7. By using concept #2, you should be able to tell when a new cycle direction is confirmed.

8. The markets differ in character from day to day. PTT's should help you trade trend days or trading range type markets.

9. The PTT's will not make the market move to them. They are guide posts or signs to help guide you on your journey.

PUBLISHER'S FOREWORD

My wife Maria and I are proud to make this book available to you, and hope that the ideas it presents will make you a more astute market analyst and a more profitable trader. It is our hope that this book will be a valuable contribution to the literature of technical analysis.

Maria and I had the good fortune and privilege to spend the better part of two days with JR Stevenson in my trading room, where he shared with us his PTT concept and showed us through many examples during the day how it worked in real time. We are grateful to him for all the time he spent with us, and feel honored to be associated with him and to help him in his goal of sharing his market knowledge with other traders.

JR's knowledge of how markets behave is truly amazing. It is, I am confident, the result of decades of close and careful study of price action. He is equally gifted in his ability to develop simple and workable methods for trading. Readers may find it of interest that, 80 years young, JR is still an active trader for his own account, concentrating on the intra-day action in the S&P E-mini market, using five minute charts. He has many other excellent ideas which he has developed over the years, which may be revealed in future books.

In order for you to employ this method, you will need access to trading software that can clone a trend line in length and slope. I was delighted to learn that the software I have used for years, Ensign, has a study called the Formations Tool which does this job nicely. JR has used Q-Charts for years in his own trading and analysis (http://www.qcharts.com) and he advises that in his opinion this is the best choice for those interested in this approach.

I wish to express my deep appreciation and gratitude to my wonderful wife Maria (who is a trader and an avid student of markets, charts, and market action) for all her help and effort in editing this manuscript and helping to prepare it for publication. She has taken a special interest in this approach and is looking forward to using it in her own market analysis, in conjunction with her own methods which she developed over years of hard work and study.

After you have studied this manual, if you have any questions concerning the methods presented, JR has graciously consented to help readers to better understand these ideas and how they may be used. He may be contacted at jstevens@midsouth.rr.com.

May the trend be with you,

Edward Dobson

Edward Dobson
Traders Press, Inc.
Greenville, SC
October, 2004

Edward and Maria Dobson

INTRODUCTION

The TOOL you are about to put in your "tool box" is so simple and easy to use that you may be tempted to discard it before trying, however "simplicity often leads to success."

In order to make a PTT [price-time target] all you need is:

1.   A charting software package that allows you to draw on trendline on a 5 minute chart (or any time frame) of an e-mini market, and to clone the trendline.

2.   Recognize by observation, the appearance of a REGULAR CYCLE and that of an INVERTED CYCLE.

3.   Connect the two cycles, again by observation, draw two trendlines and the price and time target PTT will be given at the end of the cloned trendline, plotted right on the chart.

There are no calculations, no expensive software needed, no formulas or complicated rules to follow and the same procedure is used on any chart of your choosing.

You can choose any length cycle you wish to trade that will give you the profit/loss ratio that suits your money management policy. This step is the only subjective decision you need to make to arrive at the PTT.

Proof of the above statements are in the pages to follow. Please read with an open and creative mind and you will be amazed as to how often near perfect results are obtained.

Perhaps even more important is the market analysis that is possible when the target is missed in price, time, or both. Many times you will be able to correctly predict the next move in the market because of a failure of the market to reach the PTT.

"My interest is in the future, because I am going to spend the rest of my life there!"

—Charles F. Kettering

THE FARMER AND THE MULE

Every day, before starting to plow, the farmer would hit the mule over the head several times with a ball bat and bring the mule to his knees. This went on day after day so finally someone asked the farmer "why do you hit the mule with a ball bat every day before you start plowing?" The farmer answered, "well, you see, I have to get his ATTENTION- then he will plow for me!"

To get your ATTENTION, you will be shown how quickly and accurately you can make a PTT [price and time target] on any chart, of any time frame as long as the chart reflects good trading volume and liquidity.

After a couple of examples, and if I still have your ATTENTION, I will give you the concepts for making PTT's (price and time targets). Many more examples will be presented, all of which have been charted since the time I decided to write about these concepts on June 27, 2003. I have used these concepts since 1974, and I have many examples of the PTT's in my files but to prove that the concepts are still valid in today's market, only charts after the June 27 starting date of this book will be used. There is no optimization and the same procedure is used in every time frame on every chart. I will not use old charts to prove that the concepts are valid. PTT's look to the future, not back in time!

Concept # 2 is a very useful tool to help determine when one cycle has ended and another one has started. This concept can be a "stand-alone" tool for trading and has produced great results on some days. Many examples will be shown of this tool.

OVERVIEW OF CONCEPTS

The concepts that will be presented, are original, and have been used to give "price and time targets" {PTT} for all future markets since 1974. These concepts were the basis of a market letter produced in the 70's and 80's called "Conti Cyclic Projections."

The concepts are to be considered as TOOLS to aid in your trading and analyzing the markets, and not a trading method. It is to be assumed that readers of these concepts have a basic knowledge of trading and have their own method of trading. Any knowledge of cycles will be helpful but should not be required in using these concepts.

In the 70's, when these concepts were founded, the PTT's were derived from paper charts, using only a "see-through ruler" and a sharp pencil. With the advent of the present charting packages and the ease of drawing lines, it was found that the very same concepts that were used on daily charts, were just as accurate when used on 1, 3, 5 and 60 minute charts. The concepts will be effective on any chart that has cyclic characteristics with enough volume to allow timely entries and exits. The same concept is used on every chart of any time period without being optimized. The concepts should be timeless for the future!

CONCEPT 1: By using two lines of the same length and slope, the PTT will be given for any length cycle that is isolated from the price action. The model used for this concept was designed to be very accurate. (Every cycle will give a time in the future when the price will be exactly at the target.) IMPOSSIBLE, OUTRAGEOUS, CAN'T BE DONE, RANDOM MARKETS, NEWS, ETC., ETC. Those are some comments that will be made. Will the projection be EXACT every time? OF COURSE NOT, nothing is perfect in the real world, BUT you will be amazed how many times the PTT's do turn out to be accurate, often to the very tic. [Proof will be presented.] Even more important is when the PTT's miss their mark, as this will often give information as to the future direction of prices.

CONCEPT 2: By using a line that has only ONE contact point with the price action, the end of one cycle and the start of another cycle can often be determined. This concept is a great help in knowing when prices will reverse and a new PTT can be made. [Proof will be given.] This concept could also be developed into a "stand alone" method of trading the markets.

3

E-Mini S&P 500 (Sep. 2003), 5 minute - QCharts ©2001 Quote.com 08/17/03 14:31:48

CHART 1

Let's assume that on this day, August 17th, 2003 at about 2:00 PM ET, we decide to put on a trade during the last couple of hours of trading. This chart is what is seen at that time of the day. You would see that the high had been made at 9:50, that a low had been made at 12:00, and that the market was trading near the high again at 14:00. Maybe the potential double top, the price action and concept #2 [explained later] would have told you to sell short. What would the PTT be? (The price target and the time it will be reached.)

1.   We mark high pt. as "B"
2.   We mark the low pt. as "C'
3.   We mark the last high as "D"
4.   We draw a TL from B to D
5.   We CLONE this TL [meaning the same length and slope]
6.   We move the cloned TL to point C and the end of the cloned TL is our PTT!
7.   Look at chart 2 for the end of trading at 16:15 ET

CHART 2

1. **NOTE:** the cloned TL between **C** and **A** is the same length and the same slope as the TL between **B** and **D**. [go ahead and measure]. The "dot" at the end of the cloned line is the PTT.

2. A **perfect** PTT both in PRICE and TIME! And a possible $400+ profit. (Notice the near perfect "sine" wave of the price action.)

3. Do I have your ATTENTION yet? Please remember that this example had not been charted on June 27 so it was not known that this example would be used.

CHART 3

This chart is an exception to the other examples as it is a <u>daily</u> chart of GE. I do not trade stocks any more so I seldom look at a stock chart. This was the first and only stock chart I looked at. It illustrates the cycle concept as well as showing that the concept is valid for stocks. In general, the PTT concept may be applied to any active market in any time frame!

1. We look at this chart about May 19, 2003 and mark the LOW point **A** at March 31.

2. We mark the HIGH point **B** at April 28 and we see some price action (key reversal day) about May 19 that might suggest a long position should be taken so we mark the low point here as **C**.

3. We draw a TL from point **A** to point **C**. (The trend is up.)

4. We CLONE this TL.(same length and slope)

5. We move the cloned TL to point **B** and the end of this TL will be the PTT for this cycle.

See chart 4 on following page for results.

6

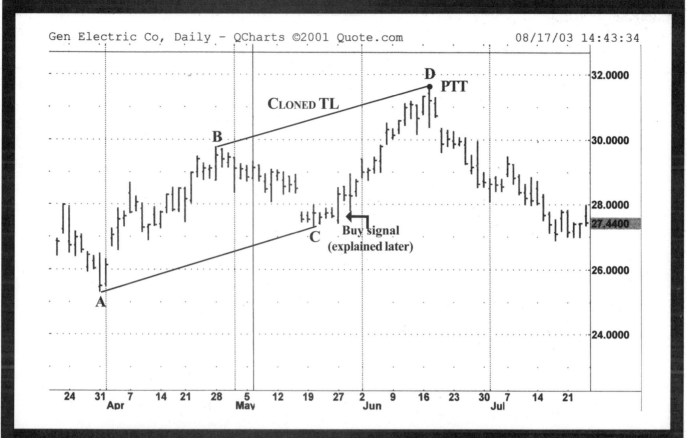

CHART 4

1. *Voila*: The end of the cloned TL is another accurate PTT. The length of the CYCLE from **A** to **C** is 36 bars, and the length of the CYCLE from **B** to **D** is 36 bars.

2. Amazing! And the PTT was known almost a MONTH in advance!

3. Now of course every PTT will not be as accurate as these two examples. You have heard many times that no one knows what the market will do in the future but you will be amazed how many times you will see near perfect PTT's, which are against tremendous odds of being that accurate just by guessing or "good luck."

REGULAR AND INVERTED CYCLES

Before showing more examples and the PTT concept, the following terms must be illustrated and explained to fully grasp the concept that will be presented.

1. In chart 1, the price action from B to D is an INVERTED CYCLE. [Starts at a high point B, has a low point C and another high point D.] The length is 52 bars.(The number of price bars between B and D.)

2. In chart 2, the price action between C and A is a REGULAR CYCLE. [Starts at a low point C, has a high point B and another low point A.] The length is 51 bars.

3. The TL that is drawn from A to C on a RC or the TL that is drawn from B to D on an IC, illustrates the trend of THAT cycle by the slope of the TL. It will be either up, down, or sideways [flat].

In order to fully understand and visualize the REGULAR and INVERTED cycles, the next two charts should help. For example: Charts 5 and 6 will show regular and inverted cycles in an uptrend. Chart #7 will illustrate what the RC and IC look like in a downtrend.

IMPORTANT: It is important to be able to recognize the RC and IC and the trend for each cycle rather quickly so orders can be entered in a timely manner.

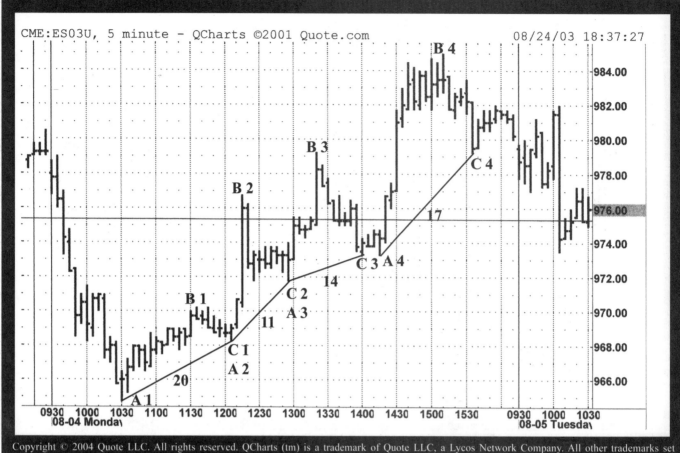

CHART 5
REGULAR CYCLES IN AN UPTREND

On Monday, August 4, 2003, there are four [4] REGULAR CYCLES [RC] illustrated on this chart.

1.   All REGULAR CYCLES in all the examples are MARKED **A-B-C**.

2.   All RC's are in an uptrend as shown by the slope of the TL drawn between **A** and **C**. RC's can be in uptrends, downtrends, or sideways trends.

3.   Note the length of the regular cycles: 20 bars, 11 bars, 14 bars and 17 bars. [The first bar is counted as #1]

There are many other regular cycles on this chart but these stand out and are clearly shown.

HINT: Notice the clear space ABOVE the TL and BELOW the price bars. This illustrates a regular cycle of "X" number of bars between two PT's **A** and **C**.

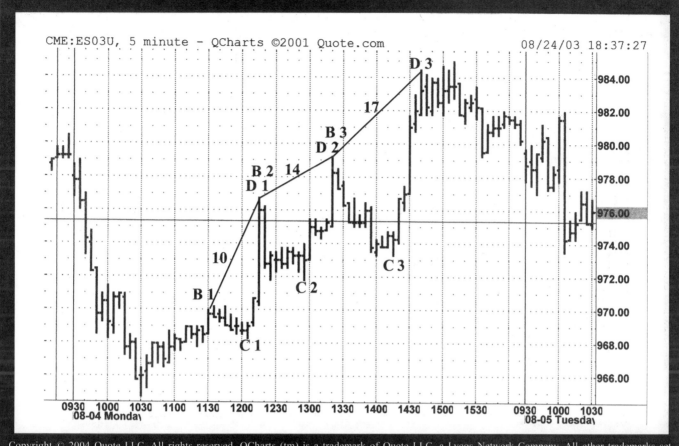

CHART 6
INVERTED CYCLES IN AN UPTREND

1. This is the same chart as the one last viewed, but only three [3] INVERTED CYCLES (IC) are illustrated.

2. All INVERTED CYCLES in all examples are marked **B-C-D**.

3. All inverted cycles are in an uptrend as shown by the slope of the TL that is drawn between point **B** and **D**.

NOTE THE LENGTH OF THE CYCLES: 10 bars, 14 bars, 17 bars. Also note the length of the RC's on the previous chart.

Notice that the clear space is BELOW the TL and above the price bars on INVERTED CYCLES. This space helps to quickly identify the IC or the RC.

There are many other inverted cycles not shown on this chart. Can you find an inverted cycle that is 20 bars in length?

HINT: Label the 10:00 bar as **B**, the 10:30 bar **C** and the 11:35 bar as **D**. Now you see the IC = the 20 bar RC on the previous page! Remember, the IC should have approximately the same number of bars as the RC.

11

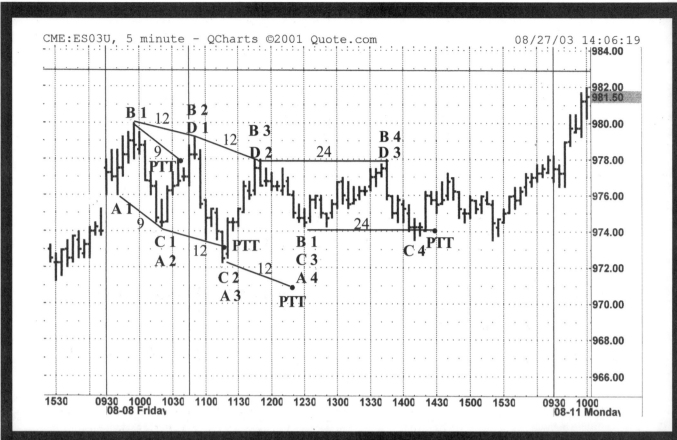

CHART 7

REGULAR AND INVERTED CYCLES IN A DOWNTREND

1. Notice the down sloping lines on the first two [2] REGULAR cycles **A-B-C**. This shows that these two cycles are in a downtrend. The first is 9 bars in length and the second is 12 bars in length.

2. Notice that there are two [2] INVERTED cycles **B-C-D** with down sloping lines. The first is 12 bars in length and the second is 12 bars in length.

3. Notice also another INVERTED cycle **B3-C3-D3** that starts at the 11:45 bar and ends at the 13:45 bar. What is the trend of this INVERTED cycle? Answer: The slope of TL between **B3** and **D3**.

4. There are many other regular and inverted cycles not marked on this chart.

5. We do not determine the PTT'S of these cycles, as at this point, as it is MORE IMPORTANT that you recognize the REGULAR and INVERTED cycles quickly and easily.

6. After the concepts are given, then you can return to this chart and determine the PTT of each cycle. Your attention should be renewed if you do this exercise.

7. Note the PTT at 12:20 ET was not reached, suggesting a stronger market, which is what developed until the close.

CONCEPT #1
PTT [PRICE AND TIME TARGET]

1.   A REGULAR cycle will ALWAYS follow an INVERTED cycle and/or an INVERTED cycle will ALWAYS follow a REGULAR cycle.

2.   The regular and the inverted cycles are expected to be approximately the same length. [Number of price bars or time.]

3.   The regular and the inverted cycle must ALWAYS be CONNECTED to each other and considered as a UNIT for a PTT. A regular UNIT is marked as **A-B-C-D** and an inverted cycle UNIT is marked as **B-C-D-A** in all the examples.

4.   A TL drawn between points **A** and **C** of a REGULAR cycle, CLONED [meaning same length and slope] and moved to point **B**, will indicate the PTT for that cycle unit [CU] at the end of the cloned TL.

5.   A TL drawn between points **B** and **D** of an INVERTED cycle, CLONED and moved to point **C**, will indicate the PTT for that cycle unit [CU] at the end of the cloned TL.

6.   MOST IMPORTANT! Expect every PTT to produce ACCURATE RESULTS, EVERY TIME in both price and time. EVERY TIME!

7.   Comment: A basketball player when shooting hoops, expects the ball to go in the hoop every time, not 50% not 90%, not most of the time, but every time. Likewise, the PTT's are expected to be correct every time, BUT of course this is not possible. However by expecting perfection, when failure comes, much valuable information can be derived as to the future direction of prices.

8.   There are many cycles and cycle units of different lengths on every chart. This concept, when fully grasped, will let the trader select the length cycle to trade, thereby choosing an acceptable profit/loss ratio that suits the trader.

9.   A PTT is for one cycle unit. The larger the selected cycle is, the more time that is needed to reach the price target. There may be one or more smaller cycle units [CU] within the larger unit. [See examples]

13

UNITS

The <u>key</u> to the PTT (price and time target) concept is understanding the concept that an IC (inverted cycle) will follow a RC (regular cycle) and that the two cycles are connected with the same price action. The two cycles will generally have about the same number of bars but this is not an absolute in the futures market due to contracts ending and in some cases trading being stopped. In an Inverted Unit the connection is between point **C** and point **D** and in a Regular Unit the connection is between point **B** and point **C**.

Another point that is difficult to grasp is that the cycles grow from one point to another. For example: from one low point early in the trading day, there might be another point 10 bars away and later in the day, another low point develops 30 bars from the first point. This 30 bar RC will become far more important in giving a larger PTT and more time to get there than the smaller cycles. Examples given should help make this point more clear. The 10 bar cycle and the 30 bar cycle may have the same starting point, but there will be 2 different PTT's plotted.

If the 30 bar cycle should develop when the 10 bar cycle ends, then there could be 3 PTT's drawn: a 10 bar PTT, a 30 bar PTT and a 40 bar PTT. There should be inverted cycles [IC's] of 10, 30 and 40 bars also.

PROCEDURE FOR MAKING A PTT IN REAL TIME

1. Inspect the last few bars on the chart for either a high point or a low point. If price is making a high point, then

2. Look back in time 15-20 (or more) bars and see if another high point has been made. If so,

3. Look for a low point between the two highs. What you have is an Inverted Cycle [IC] **B-C-D**.

4. Draw a TL between **B** and **D**, CLONE it and move to the low point **C** and the time and price at the end of the cloned TL will be the target!

OR

1. If the price in going down and appears to be making a low point then

2. Look back in time 15-20 (or more) bars and see if another low point has been made. If so,

3. Look for a high point between these two lows. What you have is a Regular cycle [RC] **A-B-C**.

4. Draw a TL between **A** and **C**, CLONE it, move it to point **B**, and the end of the cloned line is the PTT.

5. NOTE: A cycle can be 3 bars or more in length but a cycle selection of less than 8-10 bars will not provide enough price movement to make the trade profitable in most cases.

6. Generally speaking, the larger the cycle selected, the more accurate the PTT will be and the more profit will be available.

IMPORTANT

If the C point of a regular cycle is penetrated downside with a close, after a new PTT has been projected, then the PTT is <u>negated</u>, and should be deleted from the chart!

If the D point of an inverted cycle is penetrated upside with a close, after a new PTT has been projected, then the PTT is <u>negated</u>, and should be deleted from the chart!

How to Trade PTT's in Real Time

As previously stated, the PTT concept is not a trading method!

1. Buy or sell as soon as the Cyclic Trend Line [CTL] is broken with a close or on the test of the CTL after a close above the CTL. See concept #2, page 21.

2. Buy or sell at the PTT, expecting a reversal at that point.

3. Continue holding the position, in line with the trend of that cycle.

4. Trade the reactions or rallies caused by the small cycles, expecting the larger cycles to give more profit.

5. USE a moving average method and enter when the moving average is moving in the direction of the PTT.

6. Trade with the trend. The PTT will always give the trend of the UNIT that you have chosen to trade.

IMPORTANT

It is strongly suggested you enter the market with your own trading method and THEN look to the PTT's to help you manage the trade. If your entry is in line with the PTT, the odds are greatly increased that your trade will be profitable. The use of stops is always advisable.

Once you become experienced in drawing the cloned TL's on the small and large cycle units, you will be able to watch and understand market action and use it to your advantage.

Remember, the PTT's are derived from pure market action so what the market gives, is what you will get. If the PTT's fall short, accept it, analyze the market, and plan the next move.

CONCEPT #2
CTL [CYCLIC TREND LINE]

This concept was discovered while working with concept # 1 as a tool to confirm when one cycle has ended and a new cycle [trend] has started. It can at times be used as a "stand alone" trading method. The proof of the validity of this concept is in the results. It was also found that the trend line is generally "tested" before the new trend starts. The fact that most technical patterns, or points of resistance or support are "tested" at least once is well known by market technicians.

Normally this concept will be used to draw a trend line from point **C** to point **D** when analyzing an inverted cycle unit to determine when the inverted cycle has ended and\or to draw a TL between point **B** and **C** to determine when the regular cycle has ended.

This concept can be used on very small cycles but more accurate results will be obtained by using it on cycle lengths of 10 or more bars Note: Examples will make this last comment more clear.

Originally this concept was called "cyclic trend line" [CTL] as it has validity in cycle analysis. What is unique in this concept is that only one point of contact of the market action with the "cloned" line is needed. The normal trend line in technical analysis requires two or more contacts to be a valid trend line. Occasionally, the cloned line will have 2 points of contact with the price action, adding confirmation to the importance of this line.

You will notice, after seeing examples that more often than not, a break of the CTL line by a close will be followed by a pull back, touching the line [test] before resuming in the direction of the breakout. Patience, waiting for this "test" will often be rewarded with some low risk entry points.

Drawing the CTL: At the extreme high of point **B** draw a line to the extreme low point at point **C**. This basic line is then cloned [meaning same slope] [length is not important]. Now slide the cloned line to the right until it touches a price bar that is the largest distance from the basic line between points **B** and **C**. When a close breaks this line, the trend direction should change. See example on the page 23.

For a change from a trend going up to a downtrend, draw a line from the extreme low price at point **C** to the extreme high price at point **D**. Clone this line and move it to the right of the base line until it touches one point that is the largest distance from the base line. When a close breaks the cloned line, the odds are high that the trend will change. See example on page 24.

NOTE: Users of this concept have found excellent entry points by the breaking of the CTL or on the retest of the CTL, often it is broken. The two minute charts often reflect some good profitable entry points with good profit potential. Stops are suggested for all entries!

CHART 8
CONCEPT 2

This is chart #4 revisited. Likewise here, to determine if the cycle from **B** to **C** had ended, a TL was drawn from point **B** to point **C**. This TL is then CLONED and shifted to the right until it touches a single price bar, as shown. A close above this TL suggests quite strongly that the cycle from **B** to **C** has ended and the first part of the regular cycle has started up.

Other examples will show this is a very valuable tool to help make timely entries or exits from the market.

Caution is suggested in drawing the basic TL too quickly on small cycles. A good rally, or correction should be present between the basic TL starting points to avoid "stopouts." A reversal or spike reversal bar is also helpful in drawing the basic TL.

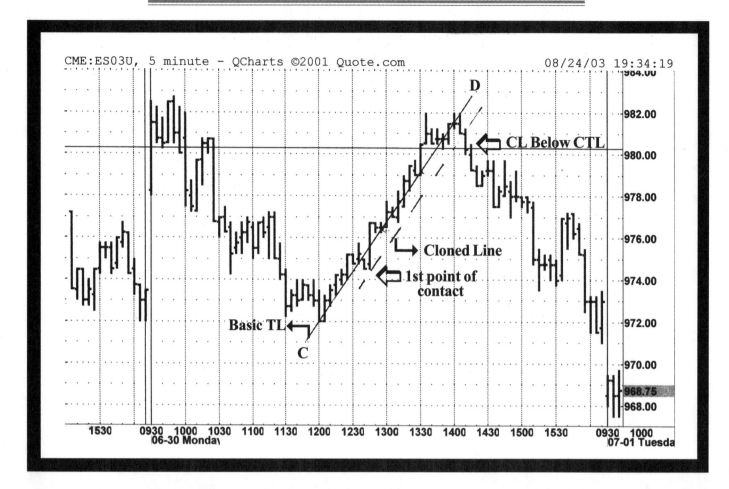

CME:ES03U, 5 minute - QCharts ©2001 Quote.com   08/24/03 19:34:19

CHART 9
CONCEPT 2

Let's revisit chart 2. We had mentioned that concept #2 might have helped you decide to go short near point **D**.

Concept 2 is as follows:

1. A basic TL is drawn between the point **C** and point **D**. [The length is not important in this concept but the slope is.]

2. This TL is then CLONED and the cloned line is shifted to the right until a price bar is touched as shown.

3. When the price closes under this trend line, the odds are high that the previous cycle has ended and the last part of the regular cycle has started.

NOTE: the TL drawn from the extreme low point **C** to the extreme high point **D** is a valid TL as it shows exactly when the TR started up and when it ended. The CLONED line therefore, by association, is a valid TL. Also, when a PT exists as at point "**D**," the basic TL should be drawn to the last bar of the PT.

HOW TO SELECT THE BEST CYCLE TO TRADE

1.   Let the market tell you!

2.   If the market has been very volatile, smaller cycles around 8-10 bars may work the best.

3.   On a rather slow moving "trading range" type market, longer cycles above 15-20 bars are more accurate and provide more profit possibilities. See chart 23 for example.

4.   Generally cycles 8 bars or less are not tradable but do provide good market analysis.

5.   To prevent over trading, select cycles 20 bars in length or more.

6.   Small cycles can be used to counter trade the trend of a larger UNIT.

7.   Try to select a cycle UNIT where the PTT will fall within the day trading hours.

8.   By dropping down to a shorter time frame, the PTT's may become more accurate and easier to observe.

HOW TO TELL WHEN A CYCLE HAS ENDED

1.   Use the CTL method or concept 2.

2.   When time and price has run out on the current cycle.

3.   Watch for certain price patterns to develop around or near a PTT.

4.   Watch for "spike reversal" or reversal bars after an extended move.

5.   Watch for volume spikes, which often develop at the PTT's, especially if a very oversold or overbought condition exists.

6.   When the momentum dries up after an emotional large move, especially if a PTT is near.

7.   After an extended move of 5-10 points, study the market swings for indication of a reversal as noted above.

WHAT IF THE PTT MISSES?

USING THE PTT AS AN ANALYTICAL TOOL: Even though every PTT is EXPECTED to be on target, both in time and price, the reality of the market place gives different results. Since there is unknown news, support and resistance levels, different trends, profit taking, sell and buy programs, and a million other reasons for trading, it is amazing that even one perfect PTT can be on target. On some days it has been observed and projected 3 or more near perfect PTT's. Of course there are many projections that do not reach the target so how can this apparent "MISS" be used to the traders advantage? Are these "MISSES" to be considered failures? Do we say the concept is worthless? Before it is thrown in the trash can, a few other interpretations will be suggested:

1.   The price target falls short in a regular cycle unit: often indicates that the cycle selected is weaker than expected and the market may decline with a possible trend change if point **C** is taken out. See chart 10.

2.   The price target falls short in an inverted cycle unit: often indicates the cycle selected is stronger than expected and the market may rally with a possible trend change if point **D** is taken out. See chart 7.

3.   In a regular cycle unit, over shooting the target, suggests a larger cycle is dominate and long positions should be held: conversely, over shooting on the inverted unit suggest a weak market and short positions should probably be held.

4.   A price target of a regular cycle that is hit early could indicate a weakening market or an accelerating market and this depends on the trend of the larger cycle in the market.

5.   A price target of an inverted cycle that comes early, could indicate a strengthening market or an accelerating trend to the down side.

6.   The time target is generally more reliable than the price targets, as trader's habits and emotions are more firmly established in the market place. To illustrate this point, notice how many cycles have approximately the same number of bars!

7.   NOTE: There are many other possibilities that exist with the PTT's. A study of the conventional cycle theory would be helpful but good observational habits should serve the trader very well.

29

BASIC QUESTIONS

The chart examples that will be shown in the balance of this manual should answer most of the following questions. You will need a chart service that allows quick and easy construction of trend lines and be able to CLONE the lines. No other tools are needed for the PTT's but I have found that a 5 bar RSI and a 10 bar moving average to be helpful and supportive at times when trading, but the indicators are not used for signals.

Q.   Do you start with a regular or an inverted cycle?
A.   See Chart 13.

Q.   How do you know when a price move [cycle] has ended?
A.   See charts 4, 5 and 16.

Q.   What length cycles should I look for to trade from a 5 minute chart?
A.   See chart 15.

Q.   How do you know which cycle will work?
A.   See chart 17.

Q.   Can a large cycle have smaller cycles within it?
A.   Yes, see chart 14.

Q.   How do you know where to start the analysis of a cycle?
A.   See chart 13.

Q.   Do I use the same length cycle throughout the day?
A.   No, the cycle lengths will expand.

Q.   Are there price patterns to look for at the turning points?

A.   See chart 8 and also page 27.

Q.   Will cycles keep me from over trading?

A.   Selecting larger cycles will reduce trading.

Q.   Is the PTT concept a trading plan?

A.   Not normally.

Q.   Is night data used for PTT's?

A.   No, because volume is not large enough.

Q.   Can the data from one day be used to find PTT's for the next day?

A.   This is not recommended for day trading.

Q.   When a CT or CB has multiple bars with the same price high or low, how is the correct point chosen?

A.   Have the TR extended to cover all the bars that are equal.

Q.   Why is perfection expected of every PTT?

A.   See page 3, "Overview of Concepts."

Q.   What do you mean when you say that a regular and an inverted cycle must be connected.

A.   See page 15, "Units."

Q.   Will knowledge of conventional cyclic theory help in working with the PTT concept?

A.   Not necessary.

Q.   How can the PTT help confirm other technical patterns that develop in the market?

A.   See chart 18.

Q.   What makes cycles work?

A.   See page 45.

Q.   Can more than one PTT be drawn at the same time?

A.   Yes, see charts 14 and 23.

Q.   What about countertrend trading?

A.   See Trading Tips on page 53.

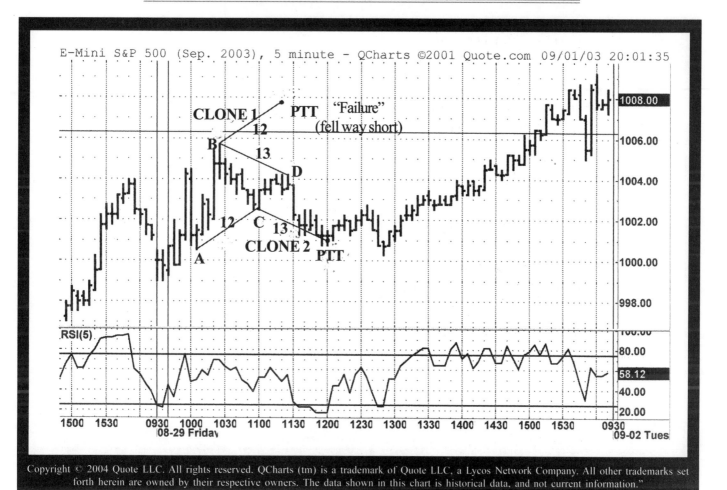

CHART 10
FAILURE AND SUCCESS

1. A trend line from **A** to **C** was drawn and then CLONED.

2. This cloned TL was attached to point **B** and the end of the TL is the PTT for the cycle.

RESULT: A high point was made at point **D** [one of the three bars] but the price target fell way short, suggesting weakness and a likely decline. Note the TR of the RC was up from **A** to **C** but the TR of the IC turned down, also suggesting a change.

3. A TL is drawn between **B** and **D** and this TL cloned.

4. This cloned line is attached to point **C** and the PTT was hit right on.

NOTE: The TL of the next smaller RC is nearly flat, suggesting that another change may be ahead. As can be seen, an 8 point rally did develop. These cycles are generally too small to trade, but they illustrate the points of "failure and success."

33

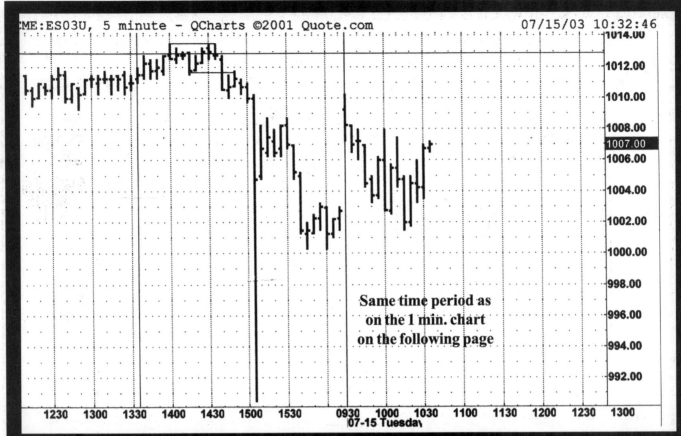

CHART 11

07/15/03 started with small cycles and rather "choppy" market action. These small cycles are not tradable but going to a one minute chart can be helpful! See next chart.

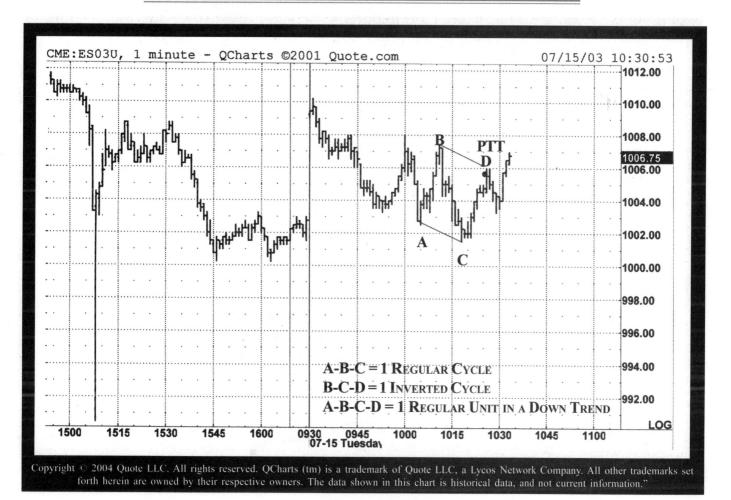

CME:ES03U, 1 minute - QCharts ©2001 Quote.com   07/15/03 10:30:53

A-B-C = 1 REGULAR CYCLE
B-C-D = 1 INVERTED CYCLE
A-B-C-D = 1 REGULAR UNIT IN A DOWN TREND

CHART 12

The regular cycle **A-B-C** gave a near perfect PTT on this 1 minute chart. **A-B-C-D** is a good example of a regular unit [RU] in a down trend. Soon after the printing of point **D**, a small regular cycle [RC] was formed with an uptrend, suggesting higher prices.

This RU was tradable as 2-3 points were possible if you had a timely entry near point **C**.

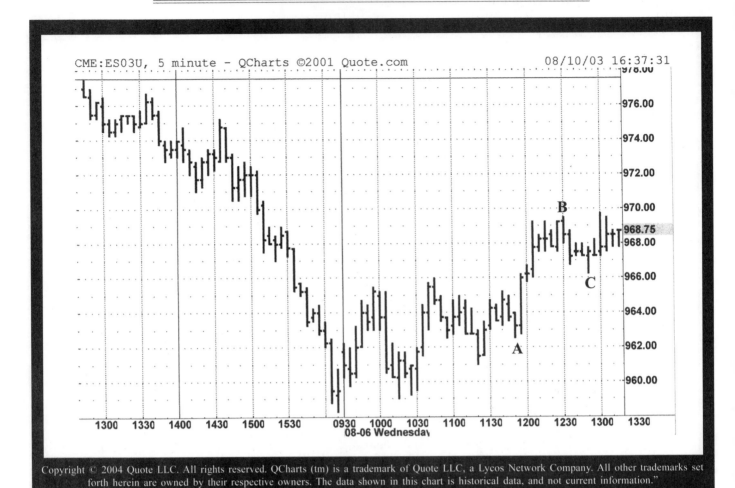

CHART 13
REAL TIME ANALYSIS FOR A PTT

At 13:15 ET this chart would be available to analyze. A quick glance would show the trend on the regular cycle [RC] [A-C] was up and there was a high point **B** between the two low points. Since all the RC since 1015 had been up and the last cycle was a RC, we would expect that an inverted cycle [IC] would follow with about the same length cycle as the RC.

A trendline was drawn from **A** to **C**, moved and then cloned to point **B**. The end of this cloned line is the PTT.

Before looking at the next chart, caution is advised to use stops because of the small double top [DT] that existed between 12:30 and 13:00. You might also note that there were 13 bars between **A** and **C**. [the first bar **A** is counted as 1].

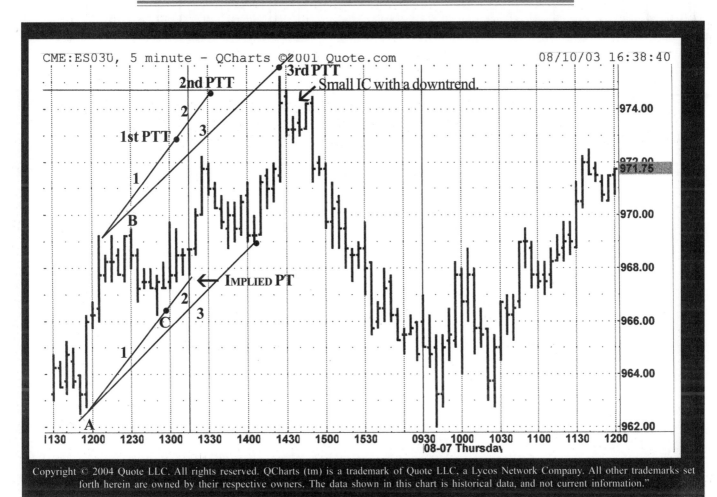

CME:ES03U, 5 minute - QCharts ©2001 Quote.com   08/10/03 16:38:40

CHART 14
RESULTS FROM PREVIOUS CHART

The first PTT [#1] fell short in price but did form a "time" point. After the first cycle ended, another small cycle formed by an IMPLIED POINT [IP] forming on the 13:15 time bar. This resulted in a large trend line [TL] from **A** to the 13:15 bar and another PTT for 13:30. This also was short but then the trend line TL from **A** to the 14:04 bar resulted in a PTT that only missed by about 2 tics.

The falling short of several PTT's soon resulted in a large decline until the close. Note the first small inverted cycle [IC] after the 3rd PTT had a downtrend, as did all the other cycles that followed.

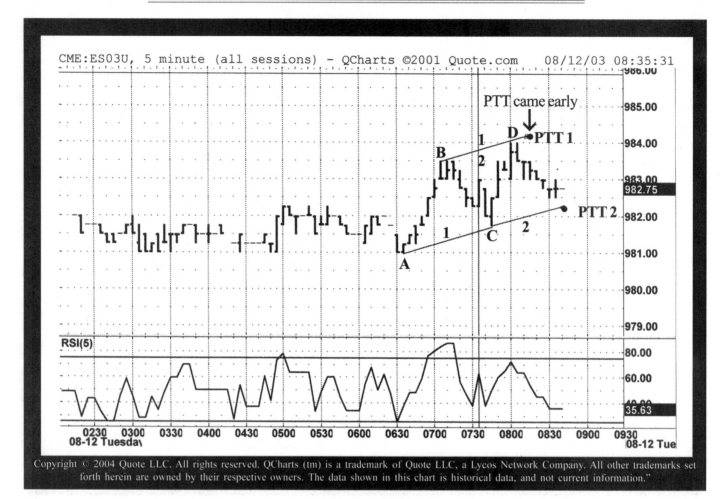

CHART 15
CYCLES IN THE PRE-MARKET CHART

There has not been enough volume in the night trading to produce good cycles or entry points. However, from time to time, I do check the "all sessions" chart as was done on 8/12/03 and a couple of good PTT's were available. The one marked 1 was made first and then CLONED. The target fell a tic short as did the 2 PTT when the chart was printed.

NOTE: The volume and liquidity in the night trading seems to be increasing, so it may develop some good PTT's in the pre-market trading. However, the data from night trading cannot be used to develop a PTT for the day session.

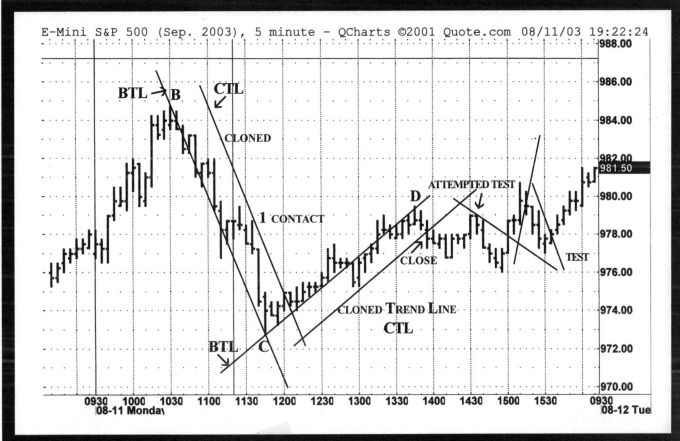

CHART 16
CONCEPT 2

A basic trend line is drawn from the highest point at point **B** to the lowest point at point **C**. This shows where the uptrend stopped at point **B** and where it stopped going down at point **C**. This basic trend line [BTL] is cloned and shifted to the right until it just touches one point on the 11:35 bar. The high point of this bar puts the cloned line the farthest from the basic line. When a close develops above this CTL, the chances are good that a new cycle has begun.

The same procedure is performed from point **C** and point **D** to tell when a down move might develop. The move did not continue far on the last CTL but with stops the trader would not have lost. The CTL's are found to be more effective on the larger cycles.

CHART 17
REAL TIME TRADING

This PTT was made in a chat room about 14:15 ET and was witnessed by 8-10 traders. The PTT was for the price to be at 994.25 by 1440, about 1 hour 25 minutes in advance. On 1440 the price was hit to the very tic and then rallied over 9 points.

Another call was made soon after the PTT for a close near 1002.50. This is another good example of how the IC is connected to the RC as the price action from **C** to **D** is the last half of the IC and also the first half of the RC from **C** to **D**.

This CONNECTION is the KEY as to why the PTT concept works so accurately.

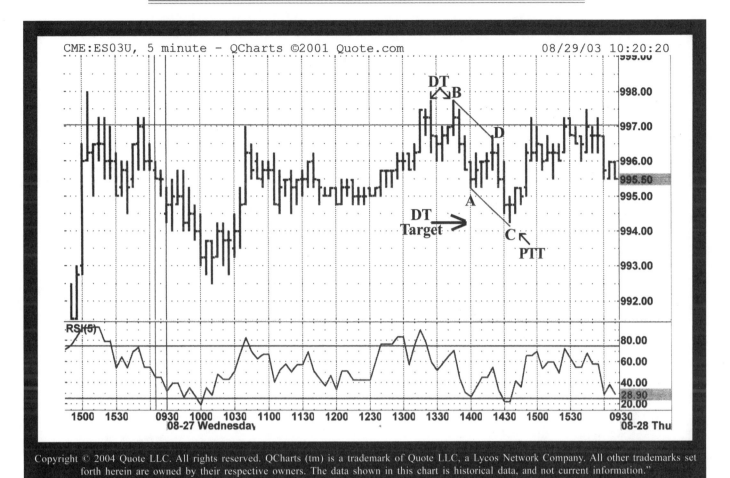

CHART 18

This call was also witnessed in a chat room. The measured target from the small double top [DT] was 994.50. After the small IC formed, a PTT was made at 994.50, the exact same price target from the DT. The PTT confirmed the DT objective! There were many other PTT's available during the day.

CHART 19
AS THE DAY PROGRESSED

The TL's marked with a number and **C** are CLONED trendlines in sequence as the day progressed. Note that the slopes of the TL's are up except for #2, which is sideways.

Note also that a PTT made from a regular unit [RU], will have an expected high and if drawn from an inverted unit [IU], the expected PTT will be a low. There are four PTT's in about 3 hours time. Could you have profited with this advance information?

Can you find the longer cycles that would give you more time to enter and to reach the PTT?

HINT: Draw a line from the 10:20 low to the 13:45 low and clone it from the high at 11:05.

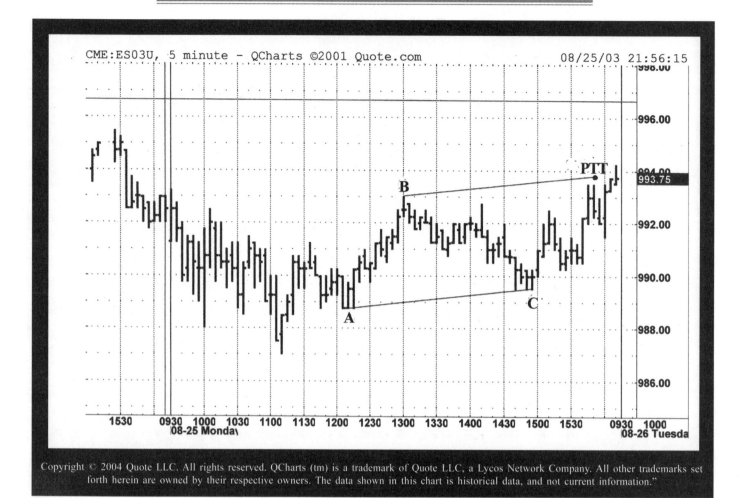

CHART 20
MULTIPLE BARS AT THE SAME CHART POINT

Point **A** has 3 bars with equal lows. Point **C** has two bars of equal lows. In a situation like this, the TL **A-C** is drawn to include all the bars, to make the line as long as possible. When the PTT is drawn the PTT should fall within the maximum length of the cloned TL. In this example the PTT fell one bar short of the TL.

In this example, the **A** starting point could have been on the 11:45 bar and the cloned line would have given a perfect PTT on the last bar of the day. It is impossible to determine which of the 4 bars at point **A** is the exact cycle low. By enclosing all of the bars, a PTT should fall within the cloned TL!

ABOUT CYCLES

What are cycles? Where do they come from? What causes them to work in the market? What is the cycle theory? Many questions like these have been asked. It is beyond the scope of this manual to discuss the conventional theory of cycles but I will try and explain a few points that may help you in using the PTT concepts.

As a starting point, some have stated a cycle is an event that repeats in a somewhat regular interval of time. For use in this manual, an event is when the price stops going up and forms a high PT or stops going down and forms a low PT. (See glossary for explanation of PT.)

Understanding the PTT concept does not require knowing the reason behind this change in EVENT. Cycles are caused by people putting in orders to buy or sell for a thousand different reasons so you would imagine that the market place would be completely random (some think it is) but careful observation suggests that habits are formed and patterns are established.

Conventional cycle theory suggests, for example, that if there is a price low [pt] every two hours, there should be another low in two more hours, which may be a larger low since it is also a four hour low. Not all cycles will have harmonics but many do.

It is also assumed that the longer a cycle is in length, that the number of points from the low to the top will be greater. This is true most often, but many small cycles can have very large amplitude, if fueled by emotion.

Cycles are not always symmetrical, that is the high does not always come half way between the two lows. Depending on the interaction of larger or smaller cycles, forming a trend, the highs may come very early or very late in the cycle. This is called "Translation." The PTT concept handles this complicated characteristic by analyzing the failure to reach the target or by the fact of reaching the target sooner then expected. [see page 29 about "WHAT IF THE PTT MISSES?"]

For further reading and study on cycles the following sources are suggested:

1. *Cycles: Selected Writings,* Edward R. Dewey
2. *How To Make Money in Commodities,* W.D. Gann
3. *The Magic of Stock Transaction Timing,* J.M. Hurst
4. Explore the many web sites containing information about cycles.

These and other books on cycles are available at **http://www.traderspress.com.**

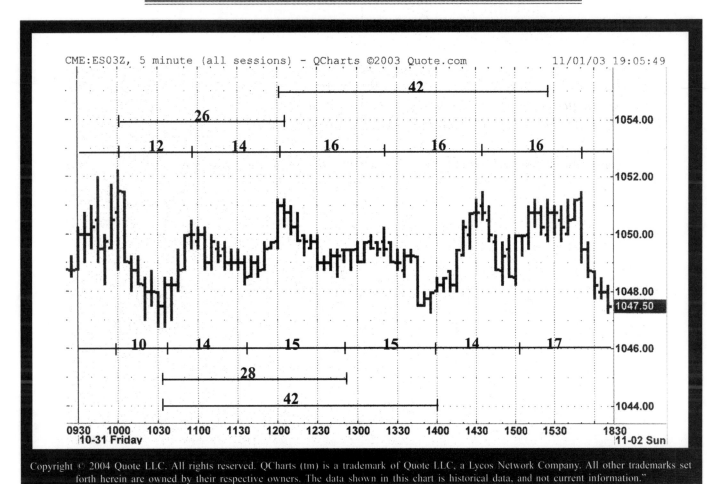

CHART 21
COUNTING BARS

The PTT concept states "A regular cycle will follow an inverted cycle and/or an inverted cycle will follow a regular cycle and each cycle unit will have approximately the same number of bars.

In the above chart of October 31, 2003, the RC lengths are shown across the bottom and the IC lengths are shown across the top.

Whether you start counting with a RC or an IC, the UNIT will have approximately the same number of bars. The longer 26 bar cycle and the 42 bar cycle also illustrate the validity of the concept statement.

When there are several bars forming a single point, including all the bars will in most cases be the correct count.

Notice that the TIME targets are often even more accurate than the PRICE targets.

Adding a price pattern requirement to the time targets might provide a timely way to enter the market at the PTT or CTL and with trend consideration.

It is suggested that the bars be counted each day for a while to confirm that RC and IC have approximately the same number of bars and that the market is not random!

47

CHART 22
GUIDANCE THROUGH THE DAY

At the 10:35 bar, the first PTT could have been drawn as shown at the end of the TL 1c. From that point on, the PTT's were drawn as the chart unfolded during the trading day. Notice the trend changing as you follow the slope of the TL on the regular cycles. Since every PTT is expected to be accurate, the "falling short" at #4 was very important in analyzing the future direction of the market.

CHART 23
CURRENT UPDATE

Since it is over a year that this manual was written, an update just before publication should be interesting, in order to confirm the concepts presented. The last completed 5 minute chart was on 10/1/04. The following points were observed:

1.   All the numberd TL's are cloned lines and the end points are the PTT's that developed as the trading day progressed.

2.   Please note the small "misses" of the PTT on lines 1, 2 and 4 which suggests a trading range developing. In fact the total range after the fast run up was only 6 points for the rest of the day.

3.   The PTT's 3, 5, 6, 7, 8 and 9, were nearly perfect as the result of concept 1.

4.   The 'Basic" TL for concept 2 was drawn at 14:10 ET, then cloned for a CTL and a buy signal was given at 14:20 for a PTT at 1132.75 to be reached at 16:05. This was hit perfectly at 16:05 and was also confirmed by the 9 PTT.

5.   Nearly every important point made in the manual over a year ago can be confirmed by the analysis of this chart. This fact should add confidence to the validity of the concepts as presented.

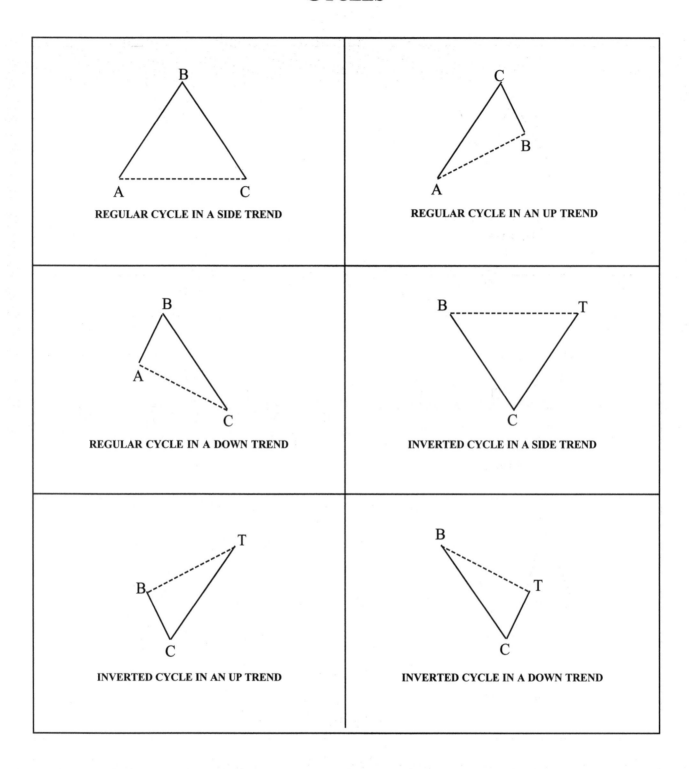

Cycles

CYCLE UNITS

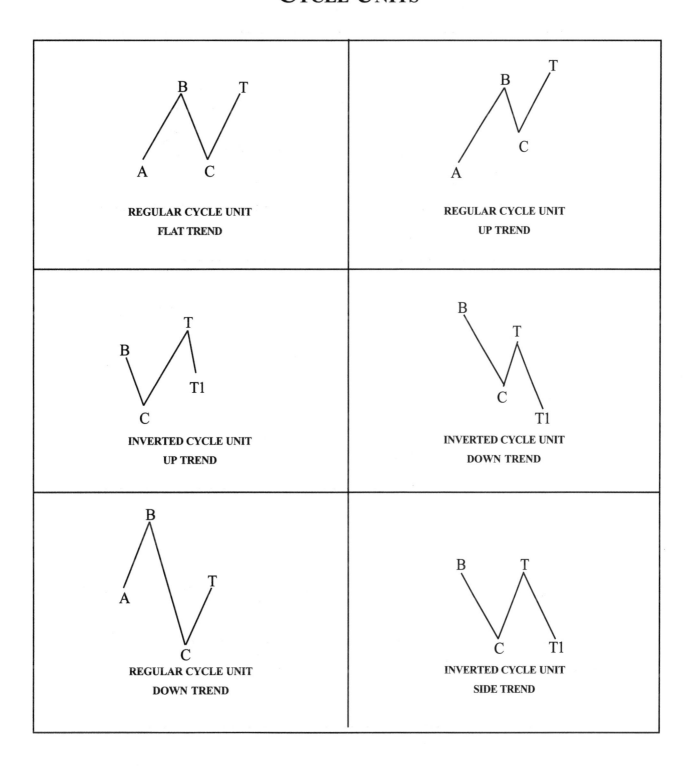

REGULAR CYCLE UNIT
FLAT TREND

REGULAR CYCLE UNIT
UP TREND

INVERTED CYCLE UNIT
UP TREND

INVERTED CYCLE UNIT
DOWN TREND

REGULAR CYCLE UNIT
DOWN TREND

INVERTED CYCLE UNIT
SIDE TREND

TRADING TIPS

If you want to trade with the trend of the cycle you selected:

> If the RC trend is up—Buy a CTL break
> If the RC trend is down—sell the PTT
> If the IC trend is up—buy the PTT
> If the IC trend is down—sell the CTL break

If you want to counter trend trade the cycle you selected:

> If the RC trend is up—sell the PTT
> If the RC trend is down—buy the CTL break
> If the IC trend is up—sell the CTL break
> If the IC trend is down—buy the PTT

Remember, the trend of the cycle you selected to trade is determined by the slope of the A-C line of an RC or the slope of the B-D line of an IC.

Many traders counter trend the markets. If you are so inclined, following the above listed tips should be of value as you will know the cycle that is being traded and when the move might be over.

POINTS OF EMPHASIS IN THIS MANUAL

1. A market truth. Derived from price bars only. No calculations, no formula, no indicators, no opinions, no bias.

2. Simplicity—drawing of two trend lines and picking the length of the cycle to trade.

3. Accuracy—If the market was a perfect sine wave, the PTT would always be correct. Of course this is not the case in real time trading. The odds of guessing where the market will trade at a time in the future would be enormous. However, the concepts produce several price and time targets through out the day that are accurate, sometimes to the very tic.

4. You must always expect a regular cycle (RC) to follow an inverted cycle (IC) or an inverted cycle (IC) to follow a regular cycle (RC) and each cycle will have approximately the same number of bars.

5. Always EXPECT the PTT's to be accurate EVERY TIME! Every miss will give analysis help.

SUMMARY

Many trading methods do not seem to work after they are sold. The PTT concepts should always be valid as long as the markets stay liquid with enough traders that form habits. The PTT's have served me well for 30 years and they continue to be valid. (See updated chart 23.)

There is no "track" record for percent right or wrong. The PTT's are derived only from the price bars and cannot be changed if the same procedure is used every time. Every PTT constructed should aid in the analysis of future market action. By plotting the PTT's on the chart as the day progresses, this should provide insight on how cycles affect the market and that the market is not random.

Good trading to all of you. If you have questions, e-mail me at jstevens@midsouth.rr.com.

J.R. Stevenson

TESTIMONIALS

"I first met J.R. Stevenson in 1981...he was my boss at my first job out of college, with ContiCommodity. I was lucky to be in a situation where I spent the first couple of years on the job learning technical and cyclical analysis from a man who, I quickly realized, had a very unique insight into market behavior. Among the techniques he taught me then was one he called cyclic projection or vectors, the Price Time Targets that this book is based on. This is the single most effective trading and analysis tool I have ever encountered, and I have never looked at a price chart since without plotting out a few of these PTT's to see where that market should go. For various reasons, I drifted away from the futures markets for a number of years, but the PTT's worked equally well in helping me with my stock purchases and sales. Recently I resumed futures trading, and immediately saw that these PTT's are just as effective and accurate on 2, 5, or 15 minute bar charts as they are on daily or weekly charts. As a reader of this book, consider yourself very fortunate that J.R. decided to share this technique with you. So enjoy this book, take the time to learn the material here, practice and get comfortable with using PTT's, and you will learn to trust them. Good trading!"
  —Reid Hampton

"Buy this manual. It is a guide to the cyclical behavior of markets and is elegant in its simplicity and accuracy. It is a method of depicting the collective behavior of market participants in both time and price and provides an invaluable complement to your current trading methodology. It is not about the psychological and money management aspects of trading. Nor is it a self-contained method of trading, although some of its principles could form the basis of a trading system. It will sharpen your trading skills and add an element of joy to your day. Happy fishing."
  —M.P.

"Thanks for your PTT manual and your assistance in applying the principles it teaches. I have been trading for more than six years and this is the most powerful tool I have ever used. I enter with my own system; however I use the PTT's as a guide to manage my trade. I am a strong believer in managing a trade in order to be a successful trader. This has increased my winnings substantially by reducing my losses and increasing my winnings. This is a must-have manual for all traders. I certainly would recommend it to anyone."
  —John Boese

"This unique method of trading is simple and easy to use. Yet it gives me valuable insights into market cycles. I am amazed that I can draw lines to precise price and time targets (PTT's) and then sit back and watch it hit precisely on that target. The PTT's coupled with the entry methods described in the manual are the most effective trading method I've found!"
  —Walt Whittington

"Just wanted to say, "Thank you, thank you, thank you!" I can't believe how simple it is! They can keep all the "fluff and stuff" market indicators. I like this simple method and will keep yours..."
  —Jo Ann Kitagawa

"Please take your crystal ball home with you over the weekend so it will be safe. Boy, you have been calling these markets great! A special thank you for the individual help you continue to give me."
  —Kathy Farrer

"Just wanted to drop you a line and tell you I, for some time now, have found your cyclic projections and analysis to be of tremendous value in my trading. I keep bar charts together with a momentum chart on seven commodities and T-Bonds. These combined with your cyclic letter are all of the inputs I want or need. Keep up the good work."
—Ed Detrixhe

"J.R., concerning your cyclic projections, I have followed Hal Cycles, MB&H, McMasters, Morgan Maxfield, James Sinclair, Bruce Gould, etc. etc. for a long time and I have found your work to be as good as any in the industry for my existing clients, as well as for soliciting new prospects..."
—John T.

"Thanks to J.R. Stevenson for his fabulous comments on the grains. All our customers appreciate his comments and this is echoed from the entire 49th trading floor in Continental Grain. As far as we're concerned, J.R. is the BEST. So if that isn't a compliment, I don't know what is. If J.R. would like to start handling some business on grains only, I believe I could find him quite a few accounts which he could manage. Many thanks for a job well done."
—Miles (former broker at Continental Grain Company)

"I'd like to take this opportunity to tell you what a fabulous job J.R. Stevenson and Reid Hampton, the Commodity Division's Technical Analysts, are doing. In my opinion they are the best thing that has happened in the firm in the 11 years that I have been here."
—Former Prudential broker

"This work is concise, well-prepared, and very understandable. The discipline they carry into their trading keeps any losses small and allows profits to run. This probably is the most difficult thing to do in futures trading. Besides having a fine grasp of the daily fluctuations in the markets, their strongest point is the ability to do an excellent job of long-term forecasting...a rather difficult task."
—Joseph A. Fineman

Partial List of Publications of Traders Press, Inc.®

7 Secrets Every Commodity Trader Needs to Know (Mound)
A Complete Guide to Trading Profits (Paris)
A Professional Look at S&P Day Trading (Trivette)
A Treasury of Wall Street Wisdom (Editors: Schultz & Coslow)
Beginner's Guide to Computer Assisted Trading (Alexander)
Channels and Cycles: A Tribute to J.M. Hurst (Millard)
Chart Reading for Professional Traders (Jenkins)
Commodity Spreads: Analysis, Selection and Trading Techniques (Smith)
Comparison of Twelve Technical Trading Systems (Lukac, Brorsen, & Irwin)
Complete Stock Market Trading and Forecasting Course (Jenkins)
Cyclic Analysis (J.M. Hurst)
Dynamic Trading (Miner)
Essentials of Trading: It's Not WHAT You Think, It's HOW You Think (Pesavento)
Exceptional Trading: The Mind Game (Roosevelt)
Fibonacci Ratios with Pattern Recognition (Pesavento)
Futures Spread Trading: The Complete Guide (Smith)
Geometry of Markets (Gilmore)
Geometry of Stock Market Profits (Jenkins)
Harmonic Vibrations (Pesavento)
How to Trade in Stocks (Livermore & Smitten)
Hurst Cycles Course (J.M. Hurst)
Investing by the Stars (Weingarten)
Investor Skills Training: Managing Emotions and Risk in the Market (Ronin)
It's Your Option (Zelkin)
Magic of Moving Averages (Lowry)
Market Beaters (Collins)
Market Rap: The Odyssey of a Still-Struggling Commodity Trader (Collins)
Overcoming 7 Deadly Sins of Trading (Roosevelt)
Planetary Harmonics of Speculative Markets (Pesavento)
Point & Figure Charting (Aby)
Point & Figure Charting: Commodity and Stock Trading Techniques (Zieg)
Private Thoughts From a Trader's Diary (Pesavento & MacKay)
Profitable Patterns for Stock Trading (Pesavento)
RoadMap to the Markets (Busby)
RSI: The Complete Guide (Hayden)
Stock Patterns for Day Trading (2 volumes) (Rudd)
Technically Speaking (Wilkinson)
Technical Trading Systems for Commodities and Stocks (Patel)
The Amazing Life of Jesse Livermore: World's Greatest Stock Trader (Smitten)
The Handbook of Global Securities Operations (O'Connell & Steiniger)
The Opening Price Principle: The Best Kept Secret on Wall Street (Pesavento & MacKay)
The Professional Commodity Trader (Kroll)
The Taylor Trading Technique (Taylor)
The Trading Rule That Can Make You Rich* (Dobson)
Top Traders Under Fire (Collins)
Trading Secrets of the Inner Circle (Goodwin)
Trading S&P Futures and Options (Lloyd)
Twelve Habitudes of Highly Successful Traders (Roosevelt)
Understanding Bollinger Bands (Dobson)
Understanding Eminis: Trading to Win (Williams)
Understanding Fibonacci Numbers (Dobson)
Winning Edge 4 (Toghraie)
Winning Market Systems (Appel)

**Please contact Traders Press to receive our current catalog describing these and
many other books and gifts of interest to investors and traders.**
800-927-8222 ~ 864-298-0222 ~ fax 864-298-0221
http://www.traderspress.com ~ e-mail ~ customerservice@traderspress.com

Trader's Gift Shop

Market-related art available through

Traders Press, Inc.®

**Varied selections of market-related
artwork and gifts are
available exclusively through
Traders Press, Inc.®
Currently available items are pictured on
our website at
http://www.traderspress.com and in our Traders Catalog,
which is available FREE upon request**

You can contact us at:
800-927-8222 ~ 864-298-0222
Fax 864-298-0221

**Traders Press, Inc.®
PO Box 6206
Greenville, SC 29606
http://www.traderspress.com